The Nightmare of Midday

Play

Seyed Ali Mohammad Razavi Tusi

Introduction

The main causes of World War II were the Mistakes of the Treaty of Versailles (May 7, 1919), which apparently ended World War I, as well as the consequences of the 1929 economic crisis and, most importantly, the political rivalry of Fascism and Western democracies and Marxism. The recent factor was so effective in the Second World War that the battle between the countries involved unleashed the public in the realm of war, so that at the end of World War II, the number of civilian and civilian deaths was almost equal. World War II, united between the two blocs of allies (Germany,

Italy and Japan) and the Allies (Britain and France, the United States and the Soviet Union), has been unique in terms of the geographic extent and destruction of human and natural resources.

The plight of the lives of the people of Germany after the defeat in the First World War and the German government's obligation to pay a heavy wartime compensation facilitated the emergence of Adolf Hitler, the main cause of the start of the Second World War. He considered Germany's defeat as a result of the conspiracy of Jews and Communists, not only calling for a revision of the Treaty of Versailles, but also with the slogan of Pan-Germanism, with the declaration of complete supremacy of the German race, the right to extend the German territory to the territory of the Slavic nations in Central Europe, and Orientalism is considered to be a rationale and racial discrimination is the basis of its worldview and has also sought to expand its influence elsewhere in the world.

On the other hand, the League of Nations made economic sanctions on Italy owing to the occupation of Ethiopia in 1935, which led to the creation of the Berlin-based Rome in 1936.

After the First World War, Britain, Russia, France and the United States possessed about 78 million square kilometers of Earth's surface (more than half the world's land). By contrast, the territories belonging to Germany, Italy and Japan totaled about 2.6 million square kilometers.

These differences reflect the determination of the prosperous countries (Britain, Russia, France, and the United States) to maintain their existing borders and avoid them from war, and also because of the growing discomfort of Germany, Italy and Japan. In the last 20 years, this led to the withdrawal of the conflict (1939-1919), the development of war tools and the spread of their territories and their militancy in the aftermath of World War II.

The occupation of Prague, the capital of Poland, was not tolerated by the German army for the Allies. The Soviet Union, which did not rely on the power of the Western governments to resist Germany, preferred to approach Germany. The

Treaty of Non-Violation of Germany and the Soviet Union on August 23, 1939 removed Hitler's fear of war on two fronts.

On September 1, 1939, the German army attacked Poland, and on September 3, Britain and France declared war on the German Reich. In less than a month, Poland defeated the German and Soviet armies and provided grounds for attacking other areas. At the beginning, Germany and its allies achieved widespread victories on all fronts in the western and eastern parts of Europe, the Middle East and the Far East. Since the fall of 1942, the situation has changed and the first signs of defeat of the allies emerged.

Occupation of the Soviet territories created an alliance with the country and provided grounds for the capture of lost lands. In late November 1942, the Soviet Red Army erupted on the eastern front, widespread counterattack in the Volga basin in the north and Stalingrad in the south, and suppressed all German forces until February 2, 1943.

The Soviet Red Army continued to advance despite the stubborn resistance of German forces in other parts of the Soviet Union, and was able to withdraw all captured lands. Thus, in the early 1943, state-driven governments had lost their initiative on all fronts. Following the British, US, and Soviet summit in Tehran (November 28, 1943), the United States and Britain were preparing an attack that was the largest military operation in World War II.

In the spring of 1944, at the same time as the joint US-British forces attacked normandy northwest, the Russians launched their large invasion in the Deniphine basin, invading Romania, Bulgaria and then Germany. On the Western Front, the US-British Joint Army, following the withdrawal of Paris on August 25, advanced to the German border, thus flooding Germany from February 1845 to the east and west.

Hitler, who was desperate to resist his underground base in Berlin, when he heard the death of Mussolini, committed suicide on April 30, 1945, and formed the new German government, the Navy's commander Donuts, in the state of Schleswig, and the Allies Demand for the conflict. On May 8, a definitive document on the unconditional surrender of Germany was signed in Berlin, and the country was divided into occupied territories based on decisions made by Roosevelt, Stalin and Churchill at the Yalta Summit in February 1945.

Three plays, titled Joseph, are the cold days of the summer, the half-day nightmares of the war triad, which is a half-day nightmare play of the third and final three.

The Nightmare of Midday

For my wife, who always helps me with patience in my hard conditions.

Light comes. Six characters in the Rook, such as chess players have. White clothes and black shadow each at the end The Rook is clear

Knight 1
  it looking at me, I know it love me.

Rook 1
  Where is this? Here? They said, came back to beach the body by water.

Pawn
  every day, in the streets, I'll be looking for it.

Rook 2
  they murdered it, doesn't? I'm guess so.

Knight 2
I want to lay on the wave of sea and don't think anymore. . .. I want to close my eyes.

Rook 1
night it's coming. Everywhere is dark.

Rook 2
Today over, what can I do with tomorrow?

Rook
Look at the water tide.

Queen
we are all ready. . . But where is the king?

Light slowly fade in the dark

Rosa's voice
I think we should finish it. I think we do not have much time.

Jack's voice
I finish it? So early?

Rosa's voice
you know; I do not like to fail.

Jack's voice
  we're always winning. Winner, do you understand?

Rosa's voice
  the winner?

Light comes. Six of Chess piece are staring at the point

Queen
  September 15, 1939

Rook 2
  the cold of Moscow.

Rook 1
  Snow is heavy. Snowflake dancing from sky.

Pawn
  It Laugh with me, It Cry with me, I know, love me.

Knight
  Look, take a good look. The sun is in the middle of the sky. Unfortunately, it's not heat again. I'm cold.

Pawn
  it not answering my call, but I know, it
  love me.

Queen
  (More serious than before) September 15,
  1939.

Rook 2
  the cold of Moscow.

Rook 1
  Snow is heavy.

Pawn
  Laugh with me. . . Excuse me, what should
  I say?

Knight 2
  I'm tired.

Light slowly fade in the dark

Rosa's voice
  you forgotten it? ... Yeah, you forgotten,
  you must understand. Look around you,
  look, take a good look. Everything given to
  you. I know, you are nothing, but you are a
  strong person. Do not worry.

Light comes

Pawn
  I'm miss it, I do not know where.

Rook 2
  we have little army. We will be defeated.

Queen
  September 15, 1939.

Rook 2
  the cold of Moscow.

Rook 1
  Snow is heavy.

Pawn
  where did I get lost? Maybe it's back.
  Sorry, I'm really sorry. what should I say?

Queen
  today is warmer than Last days.

Pawn
  but I'm cool.

Queen
  I said today is warmer than Last days.

Pawn
  I cannot.

Knight 2
  why should we continue to do this?

Queen
  Because I want.

Rook 1
  everyone by the order of Queen.

Knights 2
  When I look at myself, I see that I have
  become too old for these things.

Pawn
  what's happened if doesn't come back?

Rook 1
  they said, came back to beach the body by
  water.

Pawn
  do not talk, do not talk. It is alive, I know
  it's alive, I feel its breath.

Knight
  we have little army, so we will be defeated.

Rook 2
  I'm cool.

Queen
  September 15, 1939.

Rook 2
  the cold of Moscow.

Rook 1
  Snow is heavy.

Pawn
  But Today is warmer than Last days.

Knight 2
  war began, soldiers are tired!

Knight 1
  Let's go ahead, fight, we'll be win.

Pawn
  I'm warm, I'm warm.

Rook two
  hang on, autumn is coming soon.

Rook 1
  winter is coming, the cold of the winter is
  overwhelming.

Queen
  we have enough purveyance?

Knights 2
  Yes, sir, everything is fit, we are already for
  winter

What do you think? Think well.

Pawn

nothing, nothing. I do not want to go any further, I get tired of these things. . . I want to go back

Rook

There is no return. You have to move, as long as you play Maid, play.

Rook 1

open your eyes, be alert. They started firing, the game started. . . Everyone is ordered by the Queen.

Light slowly gives way to darkness

Jack's voice

I cannot, I cannot. . . Do not, do not, and do not accept, if I do not want to.

Rosa's voice

you grew up, you became a man for yourself. Why you don't understand, your mind is full of thirst.

Jack's voice

I'm not ready. Not to be, trust me.

Rosa's voice
do not you get ready? You should not
accept this fucking responsibility. Did you
think When you're having fun?

Jack's voice
I didn't think.

*The light comes. Sealed chess pieces
standing on the screen*

Queen
September 15, 1942.

Rook 1
(Look at the audience) Soldiers are tired.

Knight 1
we did not go so well.

Rook 2
The Red Army on that side and the Nazis
on other side.

Knight 2
what am I doing here?

Queen
this is the end, be strong. King will be sad
when we'll fail.

Pawn

  We fail every day and play again ... but it's
  ...

Rook 1

  Everyone by the order of the Queen.

Knight 1

  my feet is Tired . . . my shoes is torn. . .
  Why do not they finish this game?!

Knight 2

  will be over, will be over, what are you
  worried about?

Knight 1

  nothing

Queen closes his eyes, as if he was in a
strange sleep

Knights 2

  I am here, I stand firmly. Do not worry.
  Finally, one day, we live in a comfortable.
  Close your eyes, listen, do you feel the
  sound of the beach? When I listen to this
  sound, I get a weird calm and feel that I am
  alive, I feel that everything is great,
  sometime I drown in my dreams, I see
  myself and you, a country does not see a

war, even for once. We have a good life. I feel we are like humans, I feel we've got skin and flesh. I wish we were human, I wish we could live.

Knight 1
No, no, no . . . I'm afraid of these people.

Rook 1
we lose our soldiers, do you understand?

Rook 2
leave they alone.

Pawn
I hear its laugh from afar, I know it's alive, it's breathes. . . It's waiting for me. It will come back. Our Army cannot fight without an Elephant.

Rook 2
(Look at the Queen who she is sleeping) Our Army even fights without Queen.

Rook 1
and, of course, they fail.

Rook two
Open your eyes, they're getting very close, now it's your turn. . . Why do you pause, Hurry up, the castle is in danger.

Knight 1
  (goes on) everything is strange.

Pawn
  I'm not going anywhere. I stay so long for
  It to come back. I stay so long for news.

Rook 2
  you can't.

Light gently gives way to darkness

Jack's voice
  I have nothing to do with politics. Maybe
  it's better to escape, maybe it's better to
  take refuge in one corner of the world. I'm
  alive at least.

*The light comes. Seals are all built and
their eyes closed. Only the elephant looks
at the corner*

Pawn
  did not come. . . I missed the news tonight.
  . . Wish my place...

Rook 2

you did not sleep yet?

Pawn

I cannot sleep.

Rook 2

do not worry, find it. It come back.

Pawn

I'm alive with her love.

Rook 2

(Laugh) we forget it finally, I know you forget it. . . maybe it is on R & R (rest and recuperation) right now.

Pawn

Maybe it's just as you say, I hope it would be happy.

Rook 2

so what are you waiting for? Let me comfort it, it is alive and it is on R & R right now.

Pawn

you do not understand anything about love.

Rook 2

yeah. I do not understand.

Pawn
you're fighting when you open your eyes.

Rook 2
you're right, you better sleep, and work does not go ahead.

Pawn
Have you ever fallen in love?

Rook 2
sleep, sleep well. The weather is cold, autumn is coming. . . Look at that courtyard tree, all leaves dry.

Pawn
you do not understand anything about love...

Rook 2
I remember this tree is always on that corner.

Pawn
you see just yourself, you do not see anyone.

Rook 2
I remember many years ago, that was a very small seedling.

Pawn
sorry for myself, sorry

Rook 2
  now it's grown up.

Pawn
  Stop, stop. This your duplicate discussions
  made piss me off.

Rook 2
  sleep time. I'm sleeping. You close your
  eyes and try to sleep.

  *Rook 2 goes to his place and closes his
  eyes. Pawn moves forward it comes to a
  point. It looks like an old tree is. Light
  slowly places itself in the dark*

The sound of the pawn
  I'm not going to sleep, I close my eyes, it
  seems like a strange force open my eyelash,
  my eyes dry, and I'm blind at least. Turn
  back. You promised never to be alone, you
  remember. You promised you be with me.
  They try to keep distance between you and
  me. They keep me Away from you. They are
  afraid we together. Turn back. I do not bear
  it anymore. Turn back...

The light comes. The beads are staged in different places. Pawn in A corner has fallen

Rook 1
  it's your turn. Move on.

Knight 2
  we are failing.

Rook 1
  move on, one of the Knights must go
  ahead, hurry up.

Knight 1
  I'm going

Knight 2
  wait, I do not like you go.

Knight 1
  their army are on my side, so I have to
  move.

Knight 2
  no, no. Let's see what decision they make.

Rook 1
  we can surprise on this side, Victory is
  near. We succeed, so let's go.

Queen

   me, why me? This is to the detriment of
the castle. The castle is in danger.

Rook

   the decision is wrong. The Queen goes
forward . . . We wish her success.

Queen goes forward

Rook 2

   why sleep?

Rook

   leave it alone, let's sleep.

Rook 2

   not a good time to sleep, you do not see
how bad the situation is.

Knight 2

   (Shake hands with great success for
Knights and look at the Queen) my lady,
you will succeed. This your warrior spirit is
commendable.

Knight 1

   I Hope.

Queen
  September 15, 1944. . . I need a stupid
  pawn. Our failure is definitive, in this way.

Rook 2
  stand up, hey you, move . . . go.

Rook
  it was awake until the morning. We fail
  without pawn.

Rook 2
  it can help us now.

Rook 1
  it needs help now.

Knight 2
  Maybe we have to cover this side.

Knight 1
  they get closer, you do something. Hurry
  up.

Queen
  Hurry up.

  Pawn opens his eyes and slowly raises

Pawn
  I'm coming forward Three houses, three
  houses (look at yourself and others) Wow,
  what a strange arrangement.

Rook 1
  soldiers is dying one by one. We are not
  losing again. My lady, they surrounded you
  ... don't give up.

Rook 2
  my lady is stronger than this.

Rook 1
  this move can change the situation, the
  loss is converted to victory with a right
  move ... I hope it goes right ahead.

Rook 2
  we done, your hope is futile.

Rook 1
  be optimistic.

Rook 2
  All my being taken by Pessimistic.

Rook 1
  you lost everything for that.

Rook 2
  what do you do with your victories?

Rook 1
Where is your mind, your thoughts, your dreams?

Rook 2
they are where you sent.

Rook 1
Do you see the beach?

Rook 2
I do not see anything.

Rook 1
Time passes very soon, look at yourself.
You have changed, you're old, you haven't
Your previous strength anymore.

Rook 2
you took everything out of me.

Rook 1
I did not do anything, nothing. . . I am not guilty.

Rook 2
Go ahead, it's time. You have been selected.

Rook 1
I was elected. I was not guilty. . . Forgive me.

Rook 2

the choice was right. You can save her.

Rook 1

I cannot even save myself... Forgive me.

Rook 2

I forgave everyone.

Rook 1

Failed. We tried, but failed. We failed. This time we also failed. I have to go out, Queen should go out. . . We go out. We got used to losing. It's not strange, we play every day and losing. But it's important that losing good, you know what? Sometime I think I'm always a loser. . . I see, what does loss mean? Do you know what? If it did not win, the loss would never be conceptualized ... If it were not king, the soldiers would lose their meaning, the power that it had shrunk. Power weakens the soldiers, the strength causing everything is small. Soldiers, they are born as soldiers and dye as soldiers. But you forgot something, you forgot that we look at them as soldiers, but every one of them can be stronger than a king, but well. . . What do I saying, I have to go, I have to go outside, it's not clear what I'm saying?

Sleep and awakening meaningless, but I'm awake, but I've fallen asleep for many years, I'm awake, but I'm dreaming every second, I'm awake, but My eyelids cannot be opened. . . forgive me. Try to forget it.

Light gently gives way to darkness

Rook's Voice
  I forgot it, for years I have forgotten everything.

Knight's Voice
  we've lost again.

Knight's Voice
  today we were weaker than ever.

Queen's Voice
  Every day we were fighting weaker than yesterday.

Knight 1 sound Voice
  we've lost a pawn, we do not have a nut for a long time.

The voice of the Knight 2 Voice
  it cannot go forward, it goes ahead and goes.

Knight 1 sound Voice
  we should to look and find it.

The sound of Knights 2 Voice
  it's lost, finding it is not easy.

Knight 1 Sound Voice
  it's coming back.

Rook 1 voice
  Look at the tide of water.

Knight 2 sounds Voice
  I do not really like to imagine that the
  corpse is on see the beach waves

Knight 1 sound Voice
  be Quiet. . . Do not wake it up.

The voice of rook 1 Voice
  it slept like that it had never been awake.

Knight 1 sound Voice
  do not hurt yourself.

Voice of Rook 1 Voice
  In this situation, we should be more
  concerned than lost it.

Light goes

Rosa's voice
you are ruling your country. Things get
messed up by a Kid governor.

Jack's voice
who was saying you manage the world
easily?

Rosa's voice
No, I probably mean you can you can ruin
everything, you make everything by shit.

Jack's voice
look, look, listen my words.

Rosa's voice
here we go, my dear King, go on.

Jack's voice
I thought about that. . . I got some results.

Rosa's voice
what results? Say those.

Jack's voice
If we start this war, we can find more
power. . . We can show us to world, we can
show all of this power, just think about it
for a moment, and think with yourself if we
destroy somewhere. Then can rule the
world.

Rosa's voice

what do you know about the war? Say it ...
At that time, you were not there, even your
father. . . I was not too, but I was in war
and politician. That's better we learn about
history. The world is still in World War II.
One hundred years old from war,
everywhere its effect is seen. Do you
understand what I say? You have to learn
from history. . . All countries, after World
War II, looking for a gun Instead of science
and culture and art, making them more
powerful every day . . . Do you know what's
going on outside on the street? How do you
know how people live? You do not know.
You are ruling your country. Maybe you
should be studying at a university now.

Jack's voice

I always hated military universities.

Rosa's voice

Well, you are right, but study history. . . At
one time, at universities, there were fields
of art and culture. Do you know what's
going on in the street now? People wear
their bulletproof vests under their clothes,
in their pockets full of cartridges and
weapons.

Light comes. Like the first Rooks of the
beads are standing up

Queen
  September 15, 1945, the war ended.

Rook 1
  all Cities are hungry

Rook 2
  Peace announced but...

Knight 1
  they destroy everything.

Knight 2
  how long should we continue?!

Rook 2
  As long as they play us, we play.

Rook 1
  the game started.

Pawn
  my eyes are very low, everything is blurry.

Queen
  Move on, we'll be win. . . No matter where

the king is, it is important that you have
me.

Rook 1
All by the order of the Queen.

Pawn
The world is black and white, the colors
are gone, everywhere dark.

Rook 2
the Move one. Was decided. The Pawn
should be the front line.

Pawn
I'll go to three steps, one, two, three

*The sound of the explosion is heard. All of
them shocked*

Pawn
what was the voice?

Queen
(Pause) 1945, Dresden was destroyed.

Rook 2
Dresden city of Germany bombed.

Rock 1

One hundred thirty forty thousand dead.

Queen

The whole city is destroyed. . . We fight.
Let's go forward.

Knight 2

finish it, finish it. This dirty game.

Queen

this is the beginning of the story, we live,
play and fight, the war began, be ready . . .
move on.

Rook 2

All by the order of the Queen.

Rook 1

we'll be fight, we'll be win.

Knight 1

Watch out, do not worry about me, as
always, I'll be save.

Knight 2

I'm worried, I cannot, I cannot, I cannot.

Pawn

is it in the bombing? Is it coming back? Is
it destroyed in Dresden? . . . Help me, I
cannot go ahead. My eyes do not see a
place, everywhere is dark, dark, dark. Help

me where are they... Why are you thinking of yourself? Help me selfish guys. I cannot go forward.

Queen
  we are near victory.

Rook 2
  this time we succeeded.

Rook 1
  what is a success?

Row 2
  We'll be win.

Rook 1
  Succeed is win?

Rook 2
  Come on please?

Pawn
  help me.

Knight 2
  I wish; I can Suicide just like humans.

Knight 1
  be strong, you were a strong Chess. You are only my hope.

Knight 2
  why do not they stop it.

Knight 1
  it'll over, we'll be living comfortable, finely.

Rook 2
  so, why did you stand

Rook
  The Queen will be upset.

Knight 2
  shut up. I want to be upset; I want to see
  what does do it.

Rook 1
  it'll may be awake.

Knight 1
  all of us are in the game, so why is it sleep?

Rook 2
  Never mind, its fine.

Rook 1
  so we play to be dismissed.

Rook 2
  As long as they play us.

Knight 2
  Then they leave us in the Recycle Bin.

Knight 1
  Do we have any further application?

Knight 2
why do not we have the right to live?

Rook 1
you're free to live.

Knights 2
so why am I prison here?

*Light slowly places its place in the dark.
The whisper of people comes out. The light
comes. There is no chess. Pawn enters*

Pawn
There are no news about him. I do not
know it where! What is it doing? A Pawn
alone is very powerful. A Pawn alone can
make a huge contribution to the troops, a
pawn with Queen is enough for a winner
troop. A Pawn can fight next to Queen. A
Pawn is more powerful than Queen. But I
do not know why it does not always give us
any attention. . . A Pawn can be the
protector of a king. We have long lost a
pawn. But no one cares about it. No one is
thinking of me. I lost my life. I have no
power without it. I got tired. A life time's
ago we playing. . . I want they throw us into
the bucket. I want everything to be done

sooner. Playing with us. They do everything what they want. I do not know why, because we do not have right of speak. Because this boundless world, Because, Not allowed to breathe. We, some Lifeless chess will be destroyed by some humans. Why no one is thinking of us. (Loud noise) Winning and losing does not make sense to me. I just want to finish this dirty game sooner.

The Knight enters

Knight 1
  I was awake and I heard you. I was awake and I was sleeping for years. I was awake and I do not sleep. . . Why are you awake? why do you want destroy yourself? How long?

Pawn
  nobody understands my pain. I can't go to sleep, but when I go to bed, I sleep with nightmares.

Knight 1
  This nightmare with me for a lifetime. Day and night, sometimes, this nightmare does

not come to us at night for us. it has become a half-day nightmare.

Pawn

it Laughing with me when I close my eyes. I know, it loves me, I know it'll be go back one day. There's no place to go.

Knight 1

So you just destroy yourself.

Pawn

I have nothing to do, but I think it's just somewhere. I wish those stupid people heard our voices. I wish could we talk to them. Let's say those, one of us is lost.

Knight 1

That's right, they are deaf but they are have eyes to see. It's been several years, they play with us. Why do not they understand a pawn is missing?

Pawn

They are understand very well. They pretend they do not understand. They are playing but they do not even think about the game. They are just looking for position, money, and wealth. They are playing but they do not understand anything. They are only accustomed to sitting every day to play game with the chess board and just move us. They do not understand anything.

Knight 1

The night I was awake, I heard them talking about the war. One hundred years since World War II, But they don't want to finish this game. It's as if you want to start this war again. You want to call it Third World War.

Pawn

what's wrong with them? It was we that we lost a nut in the Second World War. It was we that we lost the original nut in that war of war. They are sitting here and thinking about themselves. Think of your ambition. It does not matter to them what the screams come up with.

Knight

I've never really understood it. The human being, who is the best of all, is in simple and everyday issues. I always feared these people.

Pawn

it's better to go to sleep. Do not bother yourself.

Knight
  With a moment, I think for just a moment, what would happen if I was where you were.

Pawn
  you're not my place, go to sleep.

Rook 1 enters the stage

Rook 1
  why do you wake up? Do not you understand the house is silent??

Knight 1
  we do not sleep. I wish the whole world was silent. I wish we did not hear the sound.

Rook 1
  this is out of the rules.

Knight 1
  what's wrong with the rules? Wake up or sounds?

Pawn
  the rules tell you a certain hour Everyone should sleep. The regulations tell you to

sleep even if you wake up. The regulations tell if you are conscious, you need to be Anesthesia. These are all castle regulations. You got it? You do not understand?

Knight 1
  We understand, but look at it. It is always the same, it has not slept for hundred years, it has not eyed a hundred years.

Pawn
  I'm going to sleep.

Pawn leaves stage

Rook 1
  Remember, according to the castle rules, you should leave this place.

Rook 1 leaves stage

Knight 1
  I wish we did not exist.

Knight leaves stage. Light brings its place to the dark

Rosa's voice
 Open your eyes. It's too early to close these. A great responsibility has been given to you. You are the leader of a country. You are the hope of a country. Be alert. You are young. You have to be careful to guide everything well. You must be careful not to sabotage. Be careful. Remember. You said, you wanted it, and never forget that you start this war. Stand hard and be strong and, at least, pretend to be a strong person. . . Remember, my father, President of the world superpower, gave you this country and he destroys him if he wants to. . . Politics.

Sound jack
 strong? I'm strong? All these fires raise your father's grave. All this posts and positions, your father gave me. Foolish politics.

Rosa's voice
 did you forget about the day you wanted to

talk to my dad? You asked. What happened now? Did you regret?

Jack's voice

  I love you and I will always love you. I want to understand that and I always take care of our common life.

Rosa's voice

  so remember, you must be responsible. You start this war because you want more power.

Jack's voice

  I did not want anything. You filled everything in my head.

Light Comes. All chess pieces are like the first scene

Knight 2

  I got tired. Why do not you finish this game?

Queen

  April 17, 2012.

Rook 2

  we are all waiting.

Rook 1
  Nostradamus's strongest prediction.

Knight 1
  the world is destroying.

Pawn
  what is the difference to us?

Queen
  April 17, 2012.

Rook 2
  we are all waiting.

Rook 1
  Nostradamus's strongest prediction.

Knight 1
  the world is destroying.

Pawn
  what should I say? Why do not you finish
  it?

Queen
  we do not die. We play and go forward.

Pawn
  (repeats coldly) we do not die. We play and
  go forward

Rook1
  we lost almost all soldiers. It's going to be harder for us all the time.

Rook 2
  This time, we should not lose.

Knight 1
  we lose every day.

Rook 2
  what is your loss for you? We are strong chess players. Look at the Queen. She is always fights stronger than yesterday.

The Queen is asleep

Rook 1
  Yes, we must be stronger than yesterday, this is part of the regulation.

Pawn
  where are we going?!

Knights 2
  my legs cannot walk anymore. My hands cannot walk anymore. T My neck cannot rotate. My face is completely numb. . . Oh, a nightmare, When will these half-day nightmares be over?

Rook 2

We play and do not scare anything. We go
ahead because they want to we go forward.
We come back because they want to we get
back. So when we are, they want to be. If
you do not, you should go in trash bin.

Rook 1

Between here and the trash, choose one.
The choice is yours.

Rook 2

Why do you think choosing with
ourselves? We are here because they want
to us be here.

Knight 2

You always keep up with these silly
discussions. Finish it. Didn't you get tired?
Take a look at outside. How small are you?
You're so small that you cannot even see
yourself. You cannot see around you too.

Queen

We are failing. Do not you understand?

Knight 2

your voice gets on my nerves. I do not
want to hear your voices. When you talk,
piss me off. Stop it. Shut up. Say a new
word. Surely we'll fail. We do not

understand. You, the Queen guide us blindly. You are not wiser than us.

The Queen is angry, goes out

Rook 2
  The Queen is upset going out.

Rook 1
  You angry the queen. I hope she forgives you.

Rook 1 leaves the stage

Rook 2
  I hope you understand your mistake.

Rook 2 leaves the stage

Pawn
  We're getting older every day. We cannot go ahead. They are fools, why do not they understand anything.

Knight 1

 Finally one day you have to face him.
You've got the right one. He cannot say
anything by virtue of his power. He cannot
do anything by his power. Thank you.
Thank you for everything.

Pawn

 I wish it was came back. No one notices
our successive failures. No one knows what
happens to us.

Pawn leaves the stage

Knight 2

 I want to live the rest of my life with you in
peace. I do not want to continue to play
this dirty game anymore.

Knight 1

 I have hope. I've always had hope and I'll
have it. Everything is great for me. I'm
happy with you. I'm happy with you both at
war and at home, I'm not leaving you even
if we are in the trash bin.

Light goes

Rosa's voice
  Look at the chessboard. These chess pieces
  are very valuable.

  My grandfather played with these chess
  pieces.

  These are all his relics. From my fathers, it
  has come to me. They are very valuable to
  me A luxury collection

Jack's voice
  I often wanted to put them all in a trash
  can we spend a lot of time on this Chess.
  It's better to buy new Chess these are all
  too old. A Pawn is lost. . .

Rosa's voice
  My grandfather said that these chess
  pieces were very valuable, he said, do not
  look at them as a chess piece. There is a
  mystery in them heart.

Jack's voice
  Your grandfather, if he was alive, He
  mocked our game with chess pieces.

Rosa's voice
  If he's alive now, He laughs at you, because

war begins tomorrow and you are sitting
here like fools and you do not do anything.

Jack's voice
  What should I do? I gave all the
  commands. Our air force is attacking five
  countries at the same time at dawn. Our
  united nations are already in the morning.
  They are ready for a clean war, and they are
  attacking several countries. We loot the
  world.

Rosa's voice
  I hope everything goes by your planning,
  because otherwise, the earth will be
  destroyed.

*Light comes. Rook 1 and Rook 2 are on
stage*

Rook1
  she said she was in love

Rook 2
  she could have said anything, why did you
  accept?

Rook1

she told me, our relationship is over. She told me, I'm not her piece.

Rook 2

She betrayed me with my sister. Look at that courtyard tree, once upon a time it was a Big tree. Look now, Dried up. a strange wind broke it Tonight. I'm sad for it. I watched that tree for A lifetime.

Rook 1

You're upset for yourself. Tomorrow, when the sun is rising from the sea, the world begins to fight. WWlll.

Rook 2

Everything in my life is dry. That tree, if not broke, was the strongest tree I've ever seen.

Rook 1

What do you say? He was the king, and whatever he wanted, we should listen to his command. We could not disregard his orders. He asked both of us and I had to accept.

Rook 2

After a century he broke with wind.

Rook

We all die one day. Tomorrow is the start of the war. It is not clear what happens to us, just pass me.

Rook 2

I look at her, I love her. I look at her and see my life, what a weird days.

Rook 1

Maybe we cannot play tomorrow anymore. Maybe this game is our last game. Probably some people are happy about this and some people not.

Rook 2

(Angrily) I love the war. I do not want to end. What can we do other than fighting? We were born warrior and die as warrior too.

Queen enters the stage

Queen

Order of the king?! Where is the king?! . . In 2045, World War III began. Green and blue disappeared on Earth and everywhere became red. . . Get up, be ready, the war began. Alert, strong and solid, moving forward, we'll win. Come on, be careful. Move on. . . We destroy them. . . (She realize that Rook 1 and Rook 2 look at her without moving, and none of the other Chess piece entered on stage. she comes slowly). . . This is the end of the tragic story of humans.

The Queen calls on everyone and the Chess piece stand in the same position as the first one. Pawn was blind and He hardly goes to his place, and after a few moments Pawn 2 arrives on the wheelchair. It stands in front of Pawn 1 and stares at it. Then goes to the empty position. Light goes. The whisper of humans is heard from afar

www.ingramcontent.com/pod-product-compliance
Lightning Source LLC
Chambersburg PA
CBHW040815200526
45159CB00024B/2990